Florida Beach Wedding Guide

A Comprehensive Beach Wedding Guide
for anticipating couples

By

Gulf Beach Weddings

DEDICATION

To the thousands of Gulf Beach Weddings
couples, mentors, and dedicated team members
who have made the last 10+ years a true delight.

TABLE OF CONTENTS

Dear Bride and Groom-to-be,

Picture it now.

The two of you are standing on a white sand beach. Turquoise waves gently lap at the shore, as the sun sets into the horizon. A gentle breeze stirs the palms as you say your wedding vows, surrounded by close family and friends.

The beach wedding you have always dreamed of, Florida's natural beauty surpassing what the most expensive interior decorator could have imagined.

At the culmination of the ceremony, just as you are saying "I do," a pair of dolphins in the distance jump out of the water, their bodies silhouetted against the setting sun. Fireworks light up the twilight sky, and Blue Angel fighter jets 'fly over' as you share your first kiss.

Between the sand, the waves, the sunset, the breeze, the fireworks, and the dolphins, it's almost as if the universe conspired to commemorate your love with the ultimate send-off. We make this happen!

-- Insert record scratch sound effect --

Is that really possible? If you are picking up this book, you may have dreamed of a beach wedding since childhood. But then the planning process begins, and you find yourself thinking, "I hear Uncle Tony does ceremonies.

Why don't we just have him do our wedding, and we can get married in the backyard. That sounds a lot easier…"

Any wedding involves a lot of moving parts but planning a beach wedding has a few elements that can make achieving that idyllic moment a challenge.

- ❖ You are often doing the preparation work from out of town and out of touch with the local amenities. Coordinating any event from miles away is tough. When it is one of the biggest days of your life, is it worth it?

- ❖ Mother Nature, when on her best behavior, can create moments like we described above. But what if she is in a foul mood?

- ❖ Even if you plan everything perfectly, what if the beach on the day of your ceremony is packed with Spring Breakers determined to break every rule their mama told them?

Those questions nag every couple, and that is the premise of this book.

We know the challenges that beach weddings pose because we most likely hold the world record for most beach weddings attended (if there was such a record).

Over ten years ago, I launched Gulf Beach Weddings®, a one-stop shop for anyone who wants to get married on the West Coast of Florida. Now, at 8,500 weddings and counting, we have literally seen it all…

❖ The bride was a no-show to the ceremony; we later found out she was arrested on her way to the wedding ceremony.

❖ Even in the middle of a hurricane when a determined couple moved their event from the beach to our Destin Warehouse for Hurricane Sally in 2020.

We've seen all the trends come and go.

But more than anything, we have seen couples realize that planning a beach wedding doesn't have to be the Olympic test of their relationship. If you have a guide, someone who can help you navigate the process, planning a beach wedding can be a lot of fun.

This book aims to be that guide.

I will walk you through the planning process, giving you tips and pointers that are targeted for the beach wedding experience. The beach environment is unique, and I want to help you tap into the beauty and the natural surroundings with wedding tips that aren't as applicable to someone getting married at a church or country club.

While there are suggestions here that should be useful to anyone getting married on the beach, we are going to focus on the stretch of coastline that I know and love: Florida's Gulf Beaches.

I will talk about the fun stuff (picking a reception venue), boring stuff (getting the marriage license) and I'll give you advice that you didn't know you needed (flower girls shouldn't throw rose petals on a cold day, unless they want to be dive bombed by seagulls).

After 10+ years in the business, I know the weather patterns, the busy traffic routes, the weekends to avoid. And...the bars to never set foot in if you want to make it to the ceremony in one piece.

I have researched and chosen the most picturesque spots for pictures, the best florists for delivering your vision and the ultimate party spots that will make your guests want to move here.

But I also know it's not just about the logistics. After saying my own vows on Coquina Beach in 2019, I know how important it is for couples to spend time preparing for marriage, rather than just planning a wedding.

As your beach wedding consultant, who has worked with more than 17,000 brides and grooms-to-be, I hope you and your future spouse use this book, but also take time to put it down. Step away from the planning, from looking at ideas on Instagram, Pinterest or Etsy and spend time talking about what brought you together in the first place.

My hope is that this book speeds up the planning process and helps you focus on preparing for life together once the reception is over and the guests have gone home.

There are some amazing tools and helpful resources located in the Appendix of this book. Even if you don't reserve with Gulf Beach Weddings®, we are happy to serve and provide this information to aid in your planning.

I can't promise dolphins if you follow my advice, but I can promise that the special day you have always dreamed of is closer than you think.

Let's get started!

Brandon J. Wheeler

Brandon Wheeler, Founder: Gulf Beach Weddings®

CHAPTER 1

Is a Beach Wedding for Me?

Here's the thing: Beach weddings are not for everyone. Before you set your sights on a beach wedding, ask yourself some questions:

❖ If you want to have hundreds of guests, dreamed of walking down the aisle in six-inch heels and you just prefer rigid formality over a good time, a beach wedding may not be for you.

❖ If you have a mother, grandmother, aunt or big sister who is going to run the show and control every element, then a beach wedding may not be for you.

❖ If your idea of a good time doesn't include lounging in the sun, enjoying the country's best beaches and reuniting with family and friends over drinks at the beach bar, a beach wedding may not be for you.

❖ If you have no interest in water sports, outdoor activities, late nights, long talks, good friends and 60–75-degree weather in January, then a beach wedding may not be for you.

❖ If you are not interested in sand between your toes and own at least one pair of sunglasses, then a beach wedding may not be for you.

In short, if you aren't that into having *fun,* then a beach wedding may not be for you.

And we get it. The idea of a beach wedding can cause a nervous bride or groom-to-be to begin thinking through all the "what-if" worst case scenarios.

What if it rains? What if it is 100 degrees? What if an errant volleyball hits the officiant in the head in the middle of your "I do's?"

But everything good in life – marriage included – requires a little bit of compromise.

A beach wedding, especially on the Gulf Coast of Florida, taps into some of nature's most stunningly beautiful backdrops. Sure, you could manipulate every element of your special day and ensure you have the exact lighting you want, but why not let the sun setting into the Gulf of Mexico be your lighting backdrop.

You could agonize over colors and matching motifs, or you could let the turquoise Gulf waters and white sand set your theme.

And you could try to micromanage the perfect event so everyone has the most fun possible, or you could just trust that, when family and friends gather in Florida to celebrate the wedding of someone they love, good times are a guarantee.

Still not sure if a beach wedding is for you? See all that apply:

- ✓ You rarely (if ever) are accused of being overly formal.

- ✓ You don't take life too seriously and get a thrill out of seeing the people around you let loose and have fun.

- ✓ You love turquoise water, dramatic sunsets, alabaster-white sand, and natural beauty over anything man made.

✓ You don't want to begin marriage with nothing in your bank account or (even worse) in debt. Use the savings to put a down payment on a new house.

By now, you are probably picking up our vibe. A beach wedding involves a certain amount of letting go, and for some couples that is not easy.

But letting go doesn't mean just rolling the dice and hoping everything turns out OK. This book can be your roadmap through that process of "letting go."

And if this book inspires you to hire the expert wedding consultant at Gulf Beach Weddings®, we are here to ensure everything will go as smoothly as possible...again, cue the jumping dolphins!

CHAPTER 2

Florida's West Coast is the Best Coast

This book should have plenty of useful insights for anyone planning a beach wedding, but we are going to focus on the West Coast of Florida, where our company, Gulf Beach Weddings® operates.

Obviously, I know Florida's left side, stretching from the Panhandle in the north to Sarasota in the south, because that is where we operate. But the real reason we are located on the Gulf Coast of Florida has to do with the award-winning beaches in every direction.

Florida's West Coast is quite possibly the best place on planet Earth to hold a beach wedding.

Bold statement? Not really, once you consider a few factors that make Florida's West Coast so unique. No hard feeling East Coasters, you are great too, but...

1 - Sunsets

If you want to see the sunset over the water without going to California or Hawaii, come to Florida's West Coast. Many couples schedule the ceremony within the sunset time frame affording beautiful wedding day photographs. Even if you have a mid-day ceremony, the perfect way to wrap up your special day is with a cocktail overlooking the water and the setting sun.

2 - Sand

Here's some geology trivia for you: Quartz rocks in the Appalachian Mountains have eroded over the millennia, tumbling into streams and rivers. Where does that quartz end up, as it gets transported south?

The Gulf Coast, where it has been transformed into some of the world's best sand. Many of the beaches where we conduct ceremonies have this fine, pure, white sand.

This white, fluffy sand is legendary, especially around the Tampa Bay region.

It doesn't get nearly as hot as darker sand, and photographers love the striking contrast that it provides for your ceremony. It is often referred to as 'sugar sand.'

Beaches on the East Coast of the state typically have tan or brown sand that is coarser underfoot.

3 - Water

The water in the Gulf Coast of Florida is known for its turquoise, Caribbean-like hue. Gulf Coast shores typically have shallow waters with sandbars. This allows the sunlight to reflect off the afore-mentioned white quartz sand, illuminating the surrounding waters. Further, up in the Panhandle, this is often referred to as the 'Emerald Coast' of Florida...yes, it's in the name!

The Atlantic Ocean has more of a brownish hue due to the deeper water just a short distance from shore (thus having a much darker color). Enough said.

4 - Waves (or lack thereof)

The Gulf Coast is mostly wave-free. This may be a disappointment for your surfer best man, but it makes for an ideal wedding spot.

You don't have to worry about guests being able to hear over the sound of waves crashing ashore, and your ceremony is not likely to be interrupted by boogie boarders or surfers.

The small waves lapping in the background are just enough to cover the footsteps where you walked. Unless it is a once-in-a-decade event, you are not likely to see any eight-foot swells crashing on the beach and upending the Bamboo Arch.

5 - The People

No offense to our friends on the Atlantic side of the state, but Florida's West Coast has a decidedly laid-back vibe. People flock to our beaches to escape the hustle and bustle of the East Coast, and they are rewarded with a far more relaxing atmosphere than you might experience in Miami or Fort Lauderdale.

There is some truth to the stereotype that Florida's West Coast is filled with friendly Midwesterners, who got here via I-75. The florists, caterers, venue managers and photographers that we work with also have that Midwestern sensibility.

6 - Pricing

The costs are generally less expensive on the Gulf Coast.

—

From Pensacola Beach to Siesta Key you'll find deals on housing, restaurants and vendors that are tough to match on the other side of the peninsula.

Why?

As Florida's population exploded over the past century, much of the growth and wealth was concentrated on the East Coast, stretching from Miami to Jacksonville. That doesn't mean the West Coast of Florida is some backwater no-man's land, but the cost of living is lower, and you can hold a beach wedding here for less.

This is expected to change as the population increases. The COVID-19 pandemic hastened the big migration south to Florida and the West Coast in particular because of the relatively lower positive cases compared to the eastern portion of the state.

But even as more and more people come to our Gulf Shores to say, "I do," our prices remain below what you will see on the other side of the state.

Convinced that the west side is the best side yet? If so...buckle up. Let's get started by talking about one of the most important issues that can also be one of the most stressful for couples who try to ignore it...the cost of saying "I do."

CHAPTER 3

The Cost of Saying "I do"

Let's start with a story about one of my favorite couples -- Susan and Jim.

Susan was thrilled when Jim got down on one knee and proposed during a weekend getaway at Lake Michigan.

The couple had dated since college, and Susan had been casually planning the wedding in her head since they first met.

She wasn't a diva or bridezilla, and she laughed when she read online that the typical wedding cost more than $33,000 in 2020.

She and Jim both had savings accounts, and her parents were chipping in a little bit, but the "typical wedding" would mean they were starting their marriage with $0 in the bank.

That number is outrageous, she thought. She wasn't envisioning a royal wedding. All she wanted was a reasonably nice event for about 90 guests.

Wedding planning consumed her life for weeks, as she began pulling the pieces together to hold a church ceremony, followed by a reception at a hotel in their hometown near suburban Chicago.

She compared florists, caterers, cake bakers, photographers, wedding coordinators and began dress shopping. Her flower budget began ballooning as she got quotes on what it would take to spruce up the interior of the church. Her photographer squashed her vision of beautiful outdoor shots in a nearby park because of the probability that it would be cold and rainy.

And as she started crunching the numbers, she realized that her allegedly low-key wedding was easily going to hit that (in our opinion) criminally high cost!

The hotel venue was charging nearly $200 per person once gratuity was included (90 x $200 = $18,000). Photography was going to be $500 per hour (3 hours x $500 = $1,500), big city pricing. Her dress was going to be $1,700. Then there were flowers ($2,000), a suit for Jim ($400), a DJ for the reception ($1,200), the cake ($500), etc, etc, etc.

In case you're not doing the math in your head, Jim and Susan's special day was already going to cost $25,300, and we haven't factored in the cost of invitations, the rehearsal dinner, the honeymoon, the engagement ring, or the time taken off work in order to coordinate the Big Day.

As she stared at her spreadsheet, Susan had an epiphany.

Why spend the equivalent of a down payment on a house on an event where she was going to have to cut corners at every turn just to stay within her budget?

That's when she called us.

Instead of the hotel wedding in the suburbs of Chicago, Jim and Susan got married for a third of the price on Anna Maria Island, one of the country's top-rated beaches.

They trimmed their guest list down to 30, keeping it to closer family and friends who they knew would love the excuse to escape Chicago and revel in the Florida sun for not just a few days, but a whole week.

Their vows took place on a Monday in November, and it was 75 degrees and sunny, while back in Chicago there was freezing rain. They had spent the weekend leading up to the ceremony lounging on the beach, playing volleyball, and hitting the beach bars that dot the Florida coastline.

They held their reception at a restaurant overlooking the Gulf, which provided a stunning backdrop as the sun set and they laughed and danced with old friends. Once everyone left to fly home, Jim and Susan stayed in Florida three more days as a built-in honeymoon or 'Wed-Cation' as we like to call it.

❖ Total cost: Under $10,000

"Our friends still talk about our wedding as one of the most fun they have ever attended," Susan said. "We didn't break the bank, and it turns out, people love an excuse to go to the beach."

Jim and Susan are a great example of stepping back, evaluating what is most important, and making decisions that reflect your priorities.

Their priorities were to (1) bring together the people they loved, (2) for a weekend they would never forget, (3) at a cost that would help (not hurt) their marriage.

(Remember we talked earlier about how marriage preparation is more important than wedding planning? Jim and Susan show us how true this is. They knew that once they got back from the honeymoon, life's demands would be waiting for them. So rather than spending every penny on wedding knickknacks they saw online, they ensured they had plenty in the bank for a down payment on a house. You can do the same.)

We have found that couples often relate to the priorities and budget decisions made by other couples. While Jim and Susan are a great example, we know that every wedding is unique. You may have read the story of Jim and Susan and found yourself nodding along.

But they are just one example of the couples we've walked through this process with.

We'll give you plenty of other examples in the next section. You and your spouse may be more of a "Scott and Linda" or "Mary and Greg."

But first, let's talk about rough dollars and cents.

Setting a budget

Before you start scoping out locations, trying on dresses or scouring Instagram for bachelorette weekend party favors, you will need to set a budget.

Set expectations: If you walk into a car dealership and say you want a brand-new car for $5,000, you won't leave a happy customer (or with a car). No matter how great a haggler you may be, you aren't going to receive a car for that price because there are certain basic costs that can't be avoided.

It's the same thing with a beach wedding. You should expect to pay anywhere from $75 to $150 per person for a beach wedding. The most bare-bones ceremony and reception still involves the beach permit, seating, an officiant, setup and teardown, and some sort of food/reception option.

Trying to go any cheaper than that, and you are likely to end up starving your guests.

The vast majority (80% or more) of our couples settle for a budget roughly in the $100 per person range for the ceremony and reception.

As we've said, a Florida Gulf Coast beach provides the world's greatest ambiance for a fraction of what you would pay at a country club or hotel, so a beach wedding is a great way to stretch those wedding dollars. And if you opt for a club or hotel, $150 per person is usually the starting point, not the high end.

One caveat to keep in mind as you read this: These rough numbers are solely for the events on the day of the ceremony. This doesn't include travel costs, buying a dress, rings, or the honeymoon. Those can widely vary depending on the couple, and we are trying to provide proven estimates for how you should approach and budget for this day, rather than a specific blueprint to follow.

The Minimal Budget: Scott and Linda

Like Jim and Susan, Scott and Linda's biggest priority was saving cash to use toward a down payment on a house.

The couple was paying for everything themselves, and they really didn't want to spend more than $3,000 for everything.

Is it even possible to have a wedding for $3,000?

Absolutely. Here is what that would look like: Our simplest ceremony on the beach runs between $1,500 and $2,000, depending on location. That leaves (roughly) $1,000 to $1,500 for the reception.

What does that get you? The day would begin with a ceremony on the beach, completely set up and run by Gulf Beach Weddings®. This includes your chairs, decor, permitting, setup and breakdown, and an officiant to preside over the ceremony.

After the ceremony, you and your guests will head over to a local restaurant of your choice, where everyone can order their dinner off the menu. Depending on the menu cost, you could even throw in one drink on the house, and then let your guests know that dinners on you but drinks are on them.

For Scott and Linda, they picked a restaurant where they knew they could stay within the $40 per-person price limit, including tax and tip.

If this is starting to sound appealing, that's because it is, particularly for couples who want a beautiful and memorable day, without breaking the bank.

Here's is Scott and Linda's general price breakdown:

The beach ceremony, put on by Gulf Beach Weddings®: $1,750

Dinner at a local restaurant for 30 people at $40 per head: $1,200 (this can be a section of the restaurant, deck, etc.)

❖ Total cost: Under $4,000

This is a great package if your top priority is your guests having fun, and you haven't been dreaming of a fairy tale ceremony since you were five years old. If your guests are likely to heckle you during an emotional speech at a formal reception, and you have a tight budget, this is the best route to go.

But keep in mind the things this arrangement doesn't include:

The ceremony will be simple. This package doesn't include bridal flowers, a live musician (recorded music is provided for the ceremony) or photographer. It will be beautiful, trust us, but simple. Your guests will be responsible for their own transportation to/from the ceremony & reception.

At the restaurant, you will be mixed in with the public, and you aren't going to be dining at Florida's finest spot. You won't have the privacy or intimacy that a private room or venue would offer. Toasting the bride and groom may be tough, depending on the size of your group and the indoor/outdoor atmosphere of the restaurant.

Remember, we aren't including travel costs, the dress, invitations, etc. *So, if you are still going to have a tough time coming in under budget, the easiest place to find savings is by lowering the number of guests.*

If a simple ceremony with a handful of close family and friends is what you are looking for, many of our couples do this with a dozen or so guests. That cuts your food bill to a third of what it would be.

Scott and Linda opted for this type of wedding. They spent just under $3,000 on their day-of events, had a great weekend with friends, and they had plenty to use toward the renovation budget on their new house.

The Middle Budget: Mary and Greg

Mary had always dreamed about her wedding day. From when she was old enough to put a pillowcase on her head and walk down an aisle of stuffed animals, she had been excited to get married.

When she and Greg began planning their ceremony, it became evident that some of Mary's childhood fantasies may have to be set aside.

It wasn't that they had to have a bargain basement ceremony in Vegas, but as they looked at vendors it became clear that there was no way they could have a string quartet at the ceremony, a tented ceremony with a live band and floral arrangements worthy of Martha Stewart. Then, they contacted us at Gulf Beach Weddings®.

They wanted the beauty, romance, and tradition of Mary's dream wedding, but wanted to stay on budget.

They went with the Wedding Dreams option that roughly 50% of our couples opt for. This is a fantastic avenue for anyone who has the cut-loose attitude that Scott and Linda did, mixed with the sentiment that says, "Hey, it's my wedding day."

For roughly $115 per person, you get the beach ceremony, complete with setup and breakdown, the chairs and officiant, along with a few vendors who are making the day extra special.

We say "vendors" because it really is up to you. Mary and Greg opted for the basic package, plus a musician to play steel drums, along with a photographer and videographer to shoot photos for an hour during and after the ceremony.

The couple ended up with a ceremony on Lido Beach near Sarasota, followed by dinner in a private room at a restaurant in St. Armand's Circle within walking distance of both the beach ceremony and their hotel.

The beach ceremony, with musician, photographer, and videographer for 30 people put on by Gulf Beach Weddings®: $3,450

Dinner in a private room at a local restaurant for 30 people at $60 per head: $1,800

❖ Total cost: $5,250

The All-Out Budget: David and Simone

David and Simone had dated for nearly a decade, so when they finally got married, they wanted it to be unforgettable.

They had been to countless weddings during their years together, in other weddings, and both made mental notes as to what they liked. They had plenty saved up for the day, but David knew from talking to friends who had married in country clubs or at hotels just how limited the options were and how quickly they could burn through their savings.

He also knew all the ways these types of venues like to fleece couples on their wedding day. He had heard horror stories of how the unexpected "fees" and "service charges" ended up costing his friends thousands.

That's what brought the couple to us.

They opted for a beach wedding on Pass-a-Grille, the south end of St. Pete Beach, with all the decor options for 70 – a steel drummer, plus two hours of photography and videography, full floral arrangements, and a champagne toast.

Instead of dinner at a restaurant, the couple rented a banquet hall with a dance floor at a private venue and had dinner catered. A DJ served as master of ceremonies, orchestrating the toasts, and dances, and the couple got the night they had dreamed of for nearly 10 years.

The beach ceremony, with all the bells and whistles, for 70 people put on by Gulf Beach Weddings®: $4,650 + $1,000 estimated custom floral arrangements

Banquet hall, catered dinner, DJ, and drinks came in at $100 per head for 70 people: $7,000

❖ Total cost: $12,650

Wrap up

These three couples are examples for you to keep in mind as you build your budget.

Jim and Susan had their priorities straight. Fun first, budget, and let's use that extra savings on our new home. All costs were borne by the couple and some serious 'DIY' options to combine the fun and limited budget on their Wed-cation with no compromising!

Scott and Linda let the natural beauty of the Gulf Beach take care of the atmosphere, and they trusted their friends could cut loose and have a memorable night without them orchestrating a formal reception.

Their priority was on saving, and with friends and family all being together in a beach town for the event, they knew good times would be had and didn't stress about the reception.

Mary and Greg fall into that middle ground that many of our beach wedding clients do. They have the independent streak that is willing to break with formal tradition, but they also want the big day to have some of the familiarity of the ceremony that they have always dreamed of. Their priority was on spending wisely, but also picking and choosing what elements they wanted.

David and Simone had been around long enough to (a) save up money for the big day and (b) know what they want and 'splurge' a little. We have several couples that also receive a stipend or some type of assistance from parents/family in this regard. This is their one and only Big Day, and they want it to be special no matter the price!

CHAPTER 4

10 Tips to Build Your Wedding Budget

1 - Have a firm bottom line

One of the first things you need to do is figure out who is going to be contributing and how much. We even recommend setting up a specific bank account for all wedding expenses. That way you can keep an eye on costs and be aware of how much you are spending.

2 - Hold the line, but treat yourself

Do your best to stay within your budget but treat yourself once. It is your wedding day, after all, so it is okay to splurge.

One couple we worked with stuck rigorously to their budget in every area -- until the groom learned that they could leave the ceremony in a vintage Rolls Royce. He was a car nut, it only cost an additional $400, and the pictures of the two-leaving turned out beautifully.

3 - Set realistic expectations

The other day, a couple called me and said they would like to have a tented reception, on the beach, with a stone crab boil. And then they added, "We are just trying to save money by not going to one of those expensive restaurants."

I tried not to laugh. What they described was at least three times as expensive as it would be to rent a private room in a nice restaurant on the water.

Spend some time researching pricing, sometimes simple costs more. In this case, the Tent Reception requires a whole layer of logistics (restrooms, ice, heating/cooling of food and guests, everything must be brought on to the beach, private property rental for 1.5 days to set up, conduct the ceremony & reception, and then take down). The list goes on...

4 - Establish priorities

As a couple, talk through what is most important to you. Is it making sure all your family and friends are there?

Is it an intimate weekend with fewer guests, but with the best food, drink, and festivities? Is it simply saving money for the honeymoon, the down payment or paying off debt?

It's important to get on the same page early in the process, and then your priorities will help guide your decision making. For example, my priority was to have as many that could come...so I was willing to make compromises in other areas (fewer custom flowers, DIY venue, etc.) to satisfy the costs for additional family in attendance.

5 - Fun is far greater than fancy

This is obviously an opinion, but we always encourage couples to prioritize fun.

There can be immense pressure to have the most Instagram-worthy ceremony and reception. And you want to have great pictures. But at the end of the day, your guests will remember how much fun they had, who they shared the experience with and not the exact shade of the chair covers or how cute the programs were.

6 - Consider making it adults only

This can be a huge cost saver, and many of your guests will appreciate it. Even if your wedding weekend is a family reunion with loads of young nieces, nephews, and cousins, you can make the reception itself adults only.

Your guests with kids will probably appreciate the night out...and it will save you the per person costs associated. To be honest, it's cute to have a dance or two with the children, certainly a flower girl/ring bearer is a nice touch. However, many couples have elected to put all the children with a local babysitter (or two) and conduct a 'Movie Night' while the parents enjoy themselves for the evening.

7 - Tipping

This is customary in the wedding industry, and you will need to tip some of your vendors. Even if the big-ticket items (restaurant, caterer, reception venue) build in an automatic gratuity, be prepared to tip the service staff.

The hotel receptionist who makes sure your flowers stay in the air conditioning until it's time for the ceremony, the bartender who puts up with your groomsmen aggressively taking advantage of the hour of free drinks, the photographer who wrangles your entire wedding party to get the perfect shots, setup crew who lug all the materials on and off the beach -- these are the key players in making sure your day is perfect.

Tip early and often, and you'll have plenty of helpers. This is certainly not required, but always appreciated!

8 - Prepare for the deposits

Most of your vendors and companies will need a deposit of roughly 25 to 33 percent.

This is an industry standard, so don't think you are being ripped off. They can't set aside their time for you and turn down other jobs without some promise of payment. Further, many vendors are hiring several other vendors for the date/time/location and permitting involved. Thus, these deposits are spent on your behalf to make sure everything is confirmed well in advance and at time of booking.

9 - The ten-five rule (economies of scale!)

For every ten guests you add, your price-per-person will go down by about 5%. Why is this important to know? Because there are fixed prices and hard costs (venue, decor, etc,) that remain the same no matter the number. Adding guests in certain areas only increases the price fractionally. It's going to cost at least $1,000 to have a beach wedding regardless of whether you have 2 guests or 20 guests. Chairs are marginally more. For example, the cost between a ceremony for 10 and 20 is not double the price (simply add chairs and coordination...call it $250 more).

Most catering and rental vendors reduce their price-per-person as you add more guests. For example, at the reception - you have already reserved the venue, decor, lighting, photographer, DJ, etc. Many of these items have economies of scale (it's the same price if you have 30 or 100). This same calculation may apply to hotel room blocks as well.

10 - The 35-person cutoff

As a rule, most restaurants can accommodate up to 35 guests. So, if you are going to have 50 people, you should be looking more towards reception venues, banquet halls, caterers, etc. not restaurants.

If you do find a restaurant willing to accommodate a large group, there may be a premium.

In the time your group is there, the restaurant likely could have flipped each table two or three times, so don't be surprised if the price per person is much more than it would be for someone walking in off the street.

Hopefully these guidelines help as you figure out where your wedding day dollars will go. Last tip -- don't fight (too much)!

Planning a wedding may be the first massive undertaking you and your partner have embarked on together. Know your limits, if you're someone who gets overwhelmed easily, allow Gulf Beach Weddings® to help you plan. Many try to do it on their own, thinking this is the most efficient and cost-effective way to proceed but end up with way more on their plate.

Consider it a practice run for all the other big and tough things you will do together -- buying a house, raising a family, making career decisions. Work on communication, sacrifice and putting the other person first.

It'll pay off down the road.

CHAPTER 5

The Two W's: When and Where

November 11, 2011 (pronounced 'eleven' 'eleven' 'eleven') was a busy day for Gulf Beach Weddings®. We performed 17 ceremonies that day, with our team running back-to-back-to-back events from Clearwater to Sarasota. While November is always a big month for us, 17 weddings in one day, plus the dozen couples we had to turn down, is unusual.

For a lot of couples, the idea of getting married on 11-11-11 was too good to resist. The same thing happened on Oct. 10, 2020, with couples wanting to get married on 10-10-20.

There are a few dates each year that really just get the mathematicians excited: 11-12-13, 12-12-12, 1-5-15, 2-2-20, 2-22-22 and the list continues...not to mention all the holiday weekends.

We made the day special for these couples, but their commitment to getting married on a specific Saturday at the peak of wedding season is not one we would recommend. It's not that you can't get married on a Saturday in spring, summer or fall – people do all the time – it's that starting with one specific date in mind throws the planning process out of whack and limits the vendor availability.

Our advice: Be Flexible (ideally have two dates in mind) or book way in advance for these unusually popular dates! Like 18-24 months...

You might get the weekend you want, but the ideal restaurant for the ceremony is already booked, there are no lodging options available, or half the vendors you had in mind are reserved.

So, as you start narrowing down your date and location, being flexible is key. Come up with a couple of dates that work. And since it's a beach wedding and you are already thinking outside the box, don't be afraid to consider a less-traditional day and time.

We do weddings more than 250 days of the year, which means more than 75% of our clients are *not* getting married on a Saturday.

Here at Gulf Beach Weddings®, we book ceremonies on a first-come first serve, and we don't vary our rates based on the day of the week (holiday's do carry a premium as it is harder to schedule and we plan for more traffic, travel, fewer vendor availability, etc.). Often companies and vendors will charge a 'weekend premium,' but with us your rate will not vary depending on the day of the week.

As you pick a date for your Gulf Beach Wedding, keep a few things in mind:

Weddings in the Tampa area run year-round. Our Weather Page has links to forecasted weather, live radar, average temperatures, and rain percentage by month. As well as hurricane probability. This is an extremely helpful tool used in the planning process.

We'll get to picking a location soon, but if you are planning an Emerald Coast wedding and will need to be between February and November. Destin is 10 to 20 degrees cooler than Tampa in the winter months, so the picture-perfect, 71-degree sunset wedding in Clearwater could be a chilly affair in the 50's with a breeze up in Destin.

Think 'mid-week'

The closer to mid-week you get, the less competition there will be for sites and vendors.

Saturdays, and Sundays are the busiest days for everyone in the wedding and food service industry, followed by Friday. If you plan your special day Monday through Thursday (on non-holiday weeks), the more likely you are to be able to lock in your top choice vendors.

Privacy

We've had couples tell us they would like a private ceremony at 5 p.m. on the Saturday of Memorial Day weekend in Destin for 150 guests. Sorry, we tell them, but that is not ever going to be possible. There are certain days and times that beaches everywhere are packed, and everything becomes more complicated (holiday weekends in particular).

The beaches are technically public, so while we do our best based on time, location, setup in advance, etc. it is very difficult to have a lot of privacy. If you are absolutely set on having the most privacy possible, we recommend private property. This could be a beach house, condo rental, etc. that is located on the 'Gulf.'

This requires written permission from the HOA, Manager, or Owner. Further, most locations like this only allow a guest count that is slightly above what the property sleeps.

For Example: if a property sleeps 18, they will allow 20-25 guests for a ceremony (not 90 Guests for a 3-bedroom house). Most rental properties also have some sort of 'clause' in the rental agreement that either prohibits special/high-traffic events or requires an additional fee charged for the additional wear and tear.

Hurricane season

Don't freak out, but Florida's hurricane season is one thing to keep in mind. It runs from June through November, with most storms materializing in the late summer months. The Tampa area seems to be somewhat more protected than the Panhandle, although it too has dodged a couple of bullets in recent years.

Since a hurricane is (a) statistically extremely unlikely but (b) completely out of your control, what should you do with this information? Well, if you know it is something you are going to worry about, consider a date in the winter or spring.

Once you have narrowed down your date to a couple of options, let's talk location.

Emerald Coast or Tampa Bay?

Here's an industry secret: All the beaches on the Gulf Coast are fantastic!

We get calls all the time from people who think we have special access to some private paradise, but the truth is that the entire coastline is dotted with beautiful spots for a ceremony. Now, we do have some seasoned insight here, however only certain locations are hand selected and suitable for a beach wedding ceremony! This is where you bring in the Pro's...

So, what we tell people is to figure out where you and your guests want to stay, and we can steer you to some great beach wedding options.

We do ceremonies out of the Tampa Bay area and the Panhandle.

If you aren't looking at a map right now, the two locales are about seven hours apart, and while they both have white sand beaches, picturesque settings and a variety of reception venues, there are some key distinctions.

Tampa Bay MSA

The Tampa Bay region is a major metropolitan area with two international airports, thousands of hotels and plenty of beaches spread throughout Pinellas, Manatee and Sarasota counties.

Whatever style of beach wedding you are looking for, you can probably find it here.

This region has everything from the classic "old Florida" opulence of The Don Cesar hotel (known as the Pink Castle), to rusty bucket dive bars, where you and your guests can drink beer and play beach volleyball.

Many of the "World's Best Beaches," ranked annually by TripAdvisor are in the Tampa region. Five area beaches cracked the top 25 in 2020, including St. Pete Beach (#1 in the U.S., #5 in the world), Madeira Beach (#5 in U.S.), Treasure Island Beach (#16 in U.S.), Siesta Key Beach (#17 in U.S.) and Clearwater Beach (#18 in U.S., previously #1 award winner too!).

The sand is white, the water is turquoise, and the sunsets are fantastic at all these spots. But the benefit of working with us at Gulf Beach Weddings® is that we know all the spots in between. And we know which of these beaches are a great place to visit, but not a great spot to hold a wedding ceremony, due to limited parking, crowds, no nearby reception venues, etc.

Tampa may be the ideal spot for you if...

❖ Many of your guests are traveling in from out of town. There is a large, international airport (TPA) and two smaller, regional airports (PIE & SRQ) within proximity of the beaches.

❖ You are open to a ceremony during the winter months (November through March).

❖ You want a huge variety of activities and amenities beyond just the beach. Between Tampa, St. Petersburg, Clearwater and Sarasota, there are plenty of museums, theme parks, sports teams and venues, and major tourist attractions for you and your guests to explore.

The Panhandle

The beaches of the Panhandle have long been one of Florida's best-kept secrets.

Destin and the surrounding beach towns are worlds away from the hustle and bustle of the rest of the State. They say in Florida, the farther north you go, the more into the South you get, and we can confirm that to be the case. If you want Florida's beautiful beaches combined with southern charm and hospitality, Destin may be the spot for you.

Destin caters more to tourists, with roughly two-thirds of the population at any time being out of towners. That means there are plenty of activities for you and your guests.

Most of the lodging is vacation rentals, beach houses and condominiums vs hotels and limited vacation rentals in the Tampa Bay area.

You may want to pick the Panhandle if...

❖ You and your guests are largely traveling by car from the Southeast or Texas

❖ Your priority is "getting away," and you don't want the distraction of a major metro area.

❖ You and your guests are going to spend most of your leisure time either hanging out on the beach or doing water sport tourist activities (fishing, sunbathing, jet skiing, boating, etc.).

❖ You want to see some of the country's most spectacular beaches. The area is known as the Emerald Coast because of the color of the water, as there are more protected beaches.

Once you have decided on Tampa or the Panhandle, check out our questionnaire to help you find your perfect beach. We know the beaches better than anyone, but before we can direct you to the ideal spot, we need to know your priorities.

If you tell us how important privacy is, how many people will attend and how close you want to be to the reception area, we can recommend some specific beaches for you.

Also, check out our Destin Beach Rating page, where we rank beaches on ideal wedding size, cost of the permit fee, how much privacy you can expect, distance to reception area, a sand rating, cost for parking and an overall rating.

Once you know the budget, you have a couple of dates, know where you want to be, and have some beaches in mind, you are getting closer to being ready to book! Give yourself a pat on the back. Your beach wedding is on its way to becoming a reality.

Lock it in!

Before you put down a deposit, give us a call to talk through your vision. While our website is designed to help guide you through the process, a wedding isn't something you throw together like an Amazon order. It always helps to get the professionals involved early because we can help you navigate the process and avoid some of the pitfalls that come when you try to go it alone.

Most restaurants and all vendors require a deposit to reserve their services and reserve the time and date. This is a wedding industry standard, and the typical deposit ranges from a flat fee to 25-33 percent of the final cost.

We handle all the vendor deposits associated with the beach ceremony when you book with us. But you will need to make separate deposits for each of the vendors as it relates to the reception and any outside vendors you reserve directly.

Couples at this point in the process can begin to feel overwhelmed because it seems like a lot of major decisions must be made at once. Picking the date, the location and then finding a reception area that all have availability can feel like assembling a jigsaw puzzle, particularly if you are doing it all from out of town.

That's why you should give us a call. We can help you navigate the process. We've had couples reserve their ceremony through our website on one of the busiest days of the year but didn't book the reception venue. By the time they got around to it, many of the best venues were already spoken for. We recommend making reservations for the reception venue at the same time as the ceremony and giving yourself the flexibility of a backup date, just in case.

CHAPTER 6

Beach Wedding Dress Code

We know that as you plan your wedding, both bride and groom will be scrutinizing Pinterest, Instagram and searching the web for the perfect wedding day ensemble. We are not going to try to give you exhaustive advice on the latest styles and trends in this chapter.

But, in the thousands of weddings we've organized, we have seen both smart and not-so-smart fashion decisions. Here are a few things to keep in mind as you pick out your outfits and tell your guests what to wear:

How formal?

You want to look nice, but you are also going to the beach.

The formality of your ceremony is generally dictated by how formal your reception is going to be and how many guests you have.

If everyone is headed to a dive bar for a night of drinking and revelry after the ceremony, you are certainly going to be less dressed up than if everyone is heading to The Don Cesar hotel, St. Pete Beach's historic "pink castle." If your ceremony just has a handful of people in attendance, most couples scale down the dress code expectations.

Footwear

Remember, the beach is sandy. This means brides want to avoid high heels or clogs. Most end up wearing simple flats, sandals or going barefoot. Most of our grooms (90%) start out with sandals but end up kicking them off and just going barefoot.

In the morning and evening, when we typically hold our ceremonies, the sand isn't as hot, and most people have no problem going barefoot. After all, we are on the beach - pretty sure the heart rate goes down a little when you're in the sand...

Groom's dress code

Most of our grooms wear a simple ensemble: Khaki pants, a button-down shirt and maybe a tie (ties are present about a fourth of the time).

Those who are going the most formal may wear a vest, but almost no one wears a jacket. Not only is it hot and doesn't breathe, but a jacket generally looks out of place during a beach ceremony.

Bride's dress code

For the bride, keep in mind that you will be navigating down a sand aisle in whatever you wear. We had one bride who, against our recommendation, insisted on a traditional 10-foot-long train. It looked lovely in pictures to start, but by the time she reached the altar she was dragging 30 pounds of sand in her train. She was a little warm and not too happy about the sweat she had worked up from her impromptu workout.

If you are going to have a full-on wedding dress, we would urge you to have a short train or one that can be pinned up, so you don't end up bringing a convoy of sand with you down the aisle.

We aren't here to give fashion advice. But brides -- we recommend keeping it simpler than you would if you were getting married indoors. The sun, breeze and sand are all factors that you should consider as you are putting together your wedding ensemble.

Bridal Hair Suggestions

Ultimately this is personal preference, and we don't want to get in the way of a bride and her perfect hairstyle. To keep it simple when you think of something outdoors, potentially warm, and windy...think 'up.' In other words, it needs to be pinned and held in place well. The more that covers the shoulders, the more it acts as a sail and doesn't let the neck breathe. I personally prefer a touch of flower (not flour), baby's breath, small sunflowers, even an orchid will add a nice touch and further the beach theme.

On several occasions over the years, the wind kicked up and was coming from the back of where the bride traditionally stands...we offered to switch the setup (so the bride faced into the wind). Little trick, but this made for a more enjoyable experience and the same great photos!

What do we tell guests?

Most people will instinctively know that a beach wedding means they should look nice, but they don't need to dress as if they are going to meet the queen.

But you may have some guests who are genuinely confused as to what to wear to your special event, so you can help them out on the invitation. Include a note that specifies the dress code.

Most of our couples opt for "polished casual." This is what you would wear for a nice night out to a restaurant where you don't need a jacket, but you also shouldn't wear jeans. For the guys, this usually leads to them wearing khakis and a button-down. Ladies tend to wear a classy sundress.

It is also good to remind your guests (you probably don't need to put this on the invitation) that they should arrive at the ceremony ready to go. Sometimes we'll have bridal parties that show up expecting to do their makeup on site. Most of the spots where we hold weddings will have restrooms, however these are your typical beach bathrooms, which have blurry mirrors and no air conditioning, the last 100 people in there were sandy and is not an ideal spot to finish getting ready.

Sunglasses

We highly recommend sunglasses for the guests but not the wedding party.

Most of our evening ceremonies use the setting sun as a backdrop. We try to situate the chairs so that the guests are not staring directly into the sun, but a pair of shades is still recommended.

For the bridal party, you should take your sunglasses off about 20 minutes before the ceremony begins. That way your eyes will have adjusted to the sun, and you will not be squinting in all the pictures.

CHAPTER 7

It's All in the Details: Flowers, Photos, Music

By this point, you are comfortable making big decisions.

You made the biggest decision of all (deciding WHO to marry). Then, decide when to get married, decide to do it at the beach, and you have picked a reception spot and food provider (more on this later).

I hope you aren't tired of making decisions. If you are, set this down, pour yourself a drink or grab a plate of brownies. We aren't done yet!

Now it's time to begin making the many small decisions that will come together to create the perfect day. We are talking about the flowers, the photos, the music and all the other details that make for a beautiful beach wedding.

Flowers

A beach wedding almost always leaves guests stunned at the natural beauty. No offense, humans, but nature is a pretty good decorator.

That is good news as you begin pulling together all the accoutrements to create a stunning setting for saying "I do." You have a gorgeous starting template, and with the right touches, you can put together an unforgettable wedding day backdrop.

Flowers are one of the first areas where you can make your ceremony and reception come alive. It is always an area where costs can begin to skyrocket. There is so much customization available, and you may begin to think that you need unique arrangements for every aspect of your ceremony. Think through how important flowers are to you as you begin talking to florists. We've worked with brides who wondered how on earth they got talked into spending more on flowers than they did on their dress, and it was mostly because they never hit pause and asked themselves, "Do I really want this?"

Our tips on getting the best flowers for your beach wedding:

1 - Hire a local Florist

If you are in Ohio planning your ceremony, Tampa and St. Petersburg look right next to each other on the map. But trust us, you don't want your florist having to cross Tampa Bay on the Howard Franklin Bridge in afternoon traffic to get your flowers to your sunset ceremony.

2 - Send the Flowers to the hotel/resort/etc.

You don't want the flowers delivered to the beach (they will wilt), and you don't want to pick up the flowers yourself (you have other things to do). Request your florist to deliver the flowers to the front desk, room, or rental property, where they can stay in the air conditioning until it is time to set up for the ceremony and in easy access.

3 - Stick with what's in Season

Out-of-season flowers are dramatically more expensive, and in-season flowers are fresher and will stay perky and hydrated longer. 'In season' is somewhat subjective as most of the flowers come from outside the US. Always best to accept recommendations from the florist for this reason.

4 - Don't micromanage the Florist

They know what they are doing, and we can connect you with the professionals who can transform your image into reality in each of the municipalities we service. Have ideas, then let the professional do his/her job.

5 – Consider Alternative Options

If you find yourself wincing as you look at the floral estimates, consider some of these alternatives:

❖ Get crafty. If you are creative and artistic, you may enjoy purchasing artificial flowers from Joanne's Fabrics®, Old Time Pottery®, Hobby Lobby® or Michaels® and making your own bouquets. You will be able to keep the arrangement as a keepsake, and for creative types it is a way to personally customize your flowers.

❖ Buy wholesale flowers and create your own arrangements. Even some of the big box retailers have a flower section (Sams Club®, Costco®, etc.)

❖ Pull double duty. Use the arrangements from your bridal party as the table decor at your reception. Just make sure your bridesmaids get the memo so that you don't have empty vases as your centerpieces.

❖ Tell the florist to use plenty of filler. Baby's Breath, greenery, etc.

❖ Some grocery stores have floral departments and employees will put together centerpieces at a discount to a florist.

Photographer – Pro Tips & Tricks, how to be a great Subject

Professing your love in front of family and friends on one of planet Earth's most beautiful beaches, you will want to capture the moment, right? Here are a few things to remember as you think about your wedding photography.

❖ A good photographer is going to be assertive, but fun. Charming, but a little pushy. And that is what you need. A photographer who can corral the wedding party with a smile is a true pro. Listen to them.

❖ You are paying for quality not quantity. In an hour, a typical photographer may shoot up to 200 pictures to find the two or three that are 'print worthy' above the mantle in your house. And typically, those shots end up being candid shots, not posed portraits.

❖ Photography time runs consecutively and is done in time blocks. You are paying for their time and expertise, including travel. This includes any down time between the ceremony and reception (Example: 4 to 8pm).

❖ You don't need every combination of guests at the ceremony. The goal of the ceremony -- when you are surrounded by nature's beauty, a setting sun, and the Gulf waters -- is to take a fair amount of group shots, combinations, however, ultimately get two or three great pictures of the couple!

❖ Don't stymie their creativity by telling them precisely what you want. Show them some examples of the style you like, look at previous work they have done, and then trust them to deliver.

❖ Most photographers will require either a half-day or full-day minimum for a wedding. If you go through one of the photographers that we use regularly, you can book them on a per-hour basis, which can really add up to some serious savings!

❖ When hiring a photographer, ask if editing and digital copies are included in their flat price or if that is extra (all of our photographers include editing in their price). Editing can dramatically improve the shots, and a good photographer can make the sunset look amazing, even on a cloudy day. In fact, the best pictures typically come on non-perfect weather days, when the sky is deep orange/blue/pink following a severe thunderstorm.

❖ The days of getting a photo album with 40 or 50 pictures are long gone. Expect the photographer to take 100-150 or so pictures per hour. The deliverables are typically 50-75% of those taken and most couples ultimately opt to get one picture blown up to put on the wall.

❖ Your photographer will most likely use a strobe, flash kit, or a bounce ring so that the subjects are lit from the front. We typically have the sun setting behind the couple, casting a shadow in front of the lens, so you need to illuminate the shadow for even lighting.

❖ Lastly, if you want photos that showcase the beauty of the day, you are going to need to hire a pro. We know everyone is a photographer these days, with cameras on our phones, but there is a dramatic difference between the shots a professional can get versus what your cousin Jimmy can get on his iPhone. There's just no phone that compares to a DSLR camera that is set to the perfect aperture given the current conditions...and post-edit in Adobe Lightroom or Photoshop (only the professionals can do this!). Even your typical indoor wedding photographer may have trouble shooting into a direct sunset without some practice. Be sure to ask this prior to.

—

Videographer

About a quarter of the couples, we work with at Gulf Beach Weddings® end up hiring a videographer to shoot their ceremony and reception. Beach weddings are so unique and have some of the best imagery for a video, if you decide to hire a videographer you may get some amazing scenery!

A few things to keep in mind:

1 – Different Skill Set

Your videographer and photographer won't be the same person. The person shooting video will be a different vendor with a different skill set than your photographer. And the two sometimes end up competing for the best positions and shots.

2 – Pricing

It can be pricey as there is much more time spent editing following the event. Expect to pay (roughly) $455 for the first hour and $250 for every hour after that.

3 – Cinematic Style

What you want is a highlight reel, not a documentary.

You won't be getting an hour-long movie that captures every single moment (your basic setup and forget it!), and that is a good thing because (literally) no one (even your mom) wants to watch your entire wedding ceremony when they come over for dinner. You will get an 8 to 12 minute video with all the key moments.

4 – Copyright Works

Don't expect to put Bruno Mars or Taylor Swift as the soundtrack. Your videographer doesn't want to get sued, so will use copyright-free music. See Appendix.

5 – Drones

Unless your videographer is a licensed drone pilot, don't expect overhead drone shots. The Federal Aviation Administration ('FAA') has cracked down on this big time. You must have a Remote Pilot Certification to fly a drone for commercial purposes. And to be honest, this is a lot of work, preparation, timing, cost and is weather dependent (low wind) for only 1-2 key shots...

6 – Microphone & Audio

To capture moments from the vows, the videographer will likely either mic up the groom or the officiant, depending on which direction the wind is coming from to minimize the static.

We provide a Microphone and PA System for groups of 50 or more automatically, so all the guests can hear. You want to avoid this addition unless necessary as it typically has static from the ocean breeze. Further, our Officiants are trained to project their voice to eliminate this need except for larger gatherings.

7 – Interview the Guests/Couple

A good videographer may do brief interviews with some of your guests to get them to offer you their best wishes. This is a fun way to get some great 'B-Roll' to your video, and it's always fun to watch years later.

Music

One of the best ways to crank the romantic beach vibe to the next level during your ceremony is with a live musician. Fortunately, you don't need to hire a string quartet or a 10-piece jazz ensemble to do that. A solo instrumentalist can create the right mood, and you won't be breaking the bank.

We recommend a steel drummer or saxophonist. Both instruments' sound carries well outdoors, and both typically cost $400-450 for an hour.

Musicians playing wooden instruments, like guitars, ukuleles or upright bassists are usually more expensive because their instruments aren't suited for the beach, and they must be amplified.

The live musician is a great touch for both your ceremony and during cocktail hour at your reception. During the ceremony on the beach, we provide a sound system, and we'll get you to choose your entrance and exit songs ahead of time.

Decor

You know you are going to have a stunning backdrop, with the Gulf of Mexico, sugar-white sand, and maybe that jumping dolphin. But some pieces of decor can really accentuate the environment's natural beauty.

One key thing we remind couples of when talking about decor is that everything, we use is commercial grade. We've had couples that wanted to make their own arch and then showed up with something so flimsy that it barely withstood a gentle breeze.

When we set up for a wedding on the beach, our team arrives two to three hours before the ceremony. This is both to allow plenty of time for setup and to shoo off any lingering sunbathers. When 99% of people see that a wedding is going to happen, they think "Oh how romantic!" and are respectful & happy to move. There is that oddball 1% who refuse to move. We know how to deal with these stubborn fellas. (Usually slipping them a five or ten-dollar bill does the trick.)

So, what does our team do when setting up for a wedding that is distinct?

1 - Rake the Sand

Our team will use lawn rakes with custom tips to smooth over the sand in the area where your ceremony will take place. This ensures that the aisle is completely smooth and ready for the bride and her bridesmaids. Our base package includes a heart in the sand, delineated with flowers. Other Wedding Packages are much more involved!

2 – Bamboo Arch Setup

Because the beach is a wide-open space, it is important to create an arbor that serves as a focal point. We will set up an eight-foot-tall bamboo arch. Under the arch is where the action takes place. It's where the bride and groom and officiant stand, providing the perfect frame for photographs of the ceremony. Our team will decorate your arch with the flowers and fabrics that you select. This provides a splash of color that contrasts nicely with the white of the bride's dress.

3 – Seating

You have three options: White Garden chairs, bamboo chairs or folding chairs with a spandex sash cover.

We have an entire palette of chair sash options and colors that is sure to satisfy every bride's taste.

4 – Tiki Torches

We'll place tiki torches extending outward from the arch. This not only directs everyone's attention up front, it also shows the bridal party where to stand (placeholder if you will). The maid of honor stands in front of the tiki torch on the left, and the best man stands in front of the torch on the right.

5 - Custom Color Palette

All our Wedding Packages include the bamboo arch, chairs, aisle way and are dressed in the colors of your choice. We use special fabrics for the arch, which are different from the chair sashes. Thus, we have an entire 'color palette' to choose from. This is how you truly make it your own...although, there's a handful of colors that are the most popular (Coral, Tiffany Blue, Navy, and Malibu Blue). When you feature the different color arch fabric alongside your preferred chair sash scheme and aisle way there are literally 8,000+ iterations. Our proprietary Beach WeddingStudio® is a great interactive tool to help you select your very own color palette and see the different color options interactively.

CHAPTER 8

Supporting Cast: Ring Bearer, Flower Girl and Pets

If you are going to be enlisting the help of children or pets for your beach ceremony, remember -- they may elicit plenty of "Awwwwww"s, but don't give them too much responsibility and be ready if they don't perform as promised.

Ring Bearer

The number one piece of advice I have for anyone using a ring bearer: Decoy, decoy, decoy.

A toddler should not be expected to carry a $7,000 ring down an aisle of sand with dozens of adults staring at him.

And unlike an indoor ceremony, if he drops the ring in the sand, it is a much tougher task -- remember, that superfine sugar sand is why you are getting married on the Gulf Coast to begin with. It can swallow a ring in no time.

Years ago, one ceremony ground to a halt five minutes in because toddler Kennedy dropped the ring (the <u>real</u> ring in the sand), the entire wedding party and guests spent the next hour looking (without success) for the ring. Not fun.

So, if you are going to have a ring bearer, buy a fake engagement ring at the dollar store, attach it to the pillow using some thread and if the adorable tyke has a meltdown and throws it into the Gulf of Mexico, no big loss. Many ring pillows come stocked with a plastic artificial version. Use it.

In addition to always using a decoy ring for the ringbearer, don't put too many expectations on children that will be involved in your ceremony. Best to have the parents nearby for some 'incentive' options to keep everything smooth and happy.

We've had couples who wanted their three children (all under the age of 5) to be pulled in a wagon down the aisle by their 9-year-old brother.

We don't tell people "No" to ideas like this -- it is your ceremony after all -- but we encouraged them to get their pictures of the kids in the wagon ahead of time, and to do a practice run to make sure the 9-year-old could handle the load.

Flower Girls

While beach weddings require a tweak to most elements of the ceremony, the flower girl is one area where not much changes. A cute little girl, walking down the aisle -- it's straightforward.

Our one piece of advice -- be careful about her tossing flower petals.

Florida birds can be similarly aggressive. When beachgoers toss food to the seagulls, it is training these loud, large birds that a human throwing 'stuff' in the air = feeding time.

So, you will want to be careful about the flower girl tossing rose petals in the air, especially if it seems like the beach is filled with birds.

We had one ceremony where an already-timid flower girl was dive bombed by seagulls as she tried to make her way down the aisle. She was not a happy camper, although I hope she one day watches the video and finds it a funny.

Further, certain locations no longer allow wedding parties to scatter rose petals on the beach, so that is one thing for you to ask us about beforehand.

Pets vs. Service Animal

More and more people are looking for ways to incorporate their beloved pooch into the ceremony. We've seen dogs as ring bearers, often with a cute vest that says, "ring security," and one fellow even had his dog stand in as his "best man."

Technically you are not supposed to have dogs or pets on any beach, but certain beach locations enforce this less than others. In our experience, if they are well-behaved, and are registered service animals you probably won't have any issue. You can get your dog registered as a service animal online before the ceremony.

As an alternative, there is a company in Tampa called Fairy Tail Pet Care® that does dog sitting for special events. If you hire them, they will come out and be your dog handler for the evening. Typically, the dog will perform some role during the ceremony, then the handler takes them, and they may make another fashionable appearance during the reception too.

If you don't hire a dog sitter, you will need to make sure someone has the sole responsibility of taking care of your dog or pet throughout the event. This person shouldn't have any key role in the ceremony. You don't want to be worried about where Lucy the lab ran off to during the reception when you should be dancing with friends.

CHAPTER 9

Being on Time is Cool

By the time your wedding comes, you will have likely spent months planning the ceremony and reception. You will have agonized over details, paid vendors hefty deposits and daydreamed about the precious moments of saying "I do" as the sun sets into the Gulf of Mexico on an idyllic sugar-sand beach.

You don't want to invest all that emotional energy and then find yourself stuck in traffic on Tamiami Trail when the ceremony is about to begin.

And you don't want to be anxiously watching the sun go down with most of the seats remaining empty because your family and friends are late.

That brings us to the most basic but most important item on everybody's to-do list on your wedding day: Get to the ceremony on time (or early!).

This may sound simple, but after more than 8,500 weddings, we know that it is not. Beach weddings have a few characteristics that make them uniquely special but also make them vulnerable to tardiness.

1 - It's the Beach, man, Relax!

The reason you picked a beach wedding is likely because you and your friends have a laid-back streak. That is great, but there is good laid back and bad laid back.

❖ Good laid back: Not being a bridezilla.

❖ Bad laid back: Not being at the ceremony because you had too much to drink at the beach bar or didn't build in a 15–30-minute buffer for traffic and parking.

2 - Beaches are Popular Places

You aren't alone in thinking the beach is your happy place.

The day of your ceremony, you and your guests will likely be competing with other beachgoers as you navigate traffic and look for parking.

It depends on the time of year and the exact spot where you are holding your ceremony, but it is extremely rare to have a completely isolated location with an empty parking lot waiting for you.

We do weddings in the same or similar wedding site's year-round, so we know where all the best parking spots are, and we can advise you specifically how much time to allow depending on where your guests are coming from. The main reason we try to avoid holding ceremonies during the 11 a.m. to 4 p.m. time frame is to avoid the crowds. Beach goers often sunbathe during the height of direct sunlight, as we move into the evening time frame, most retreat to other planned activities - leaving us the perfect backdrop for your Big Day.

3 - Guests are most likely out-of-towners

Most of the couples that we do ceremonies for do not live on the Gulf Coast of Florida. That means both the couple and their guests are navigating a new town.

So, what can you do ahead of time to make sure your guests make it to the ceremony on time?

❖ You know your guests. Some people will see that a wedding starts at 5pm, and that means they will be pulling into the parking lot at 5:05pm.

Others know that when a wedding starts at 5 p.m., that means they should be seated by 4:45. You may need to tell some guests that the ceremony starts 30 minutes earlier than it actually will. Some even put it in the Invitation or Program that way.

❖ Build in buffers. Assume it is going to take 10 to 15 minutes to get everyone loaded into cars, assume you will hit traffic and assume it will take 10 to 15 minutes to find a parking space. If the ceremony is a 15-minute drive away from the hotel, everyone should be walking out of the hotel room, dressed and ready to go, 50 minutes before your target arrival time.

❖ Give people landmarks. There are no addresses on the beach, so be as specific as possible when telling your guests where to go. Aerials on the Gulf Beach Weddings® website is very helpful. Other helpful hints ('End of 22nd Ave,' 'Rock Jetty,' 'Straight out from the Boardwalk 29B,' etc.)

❖ Try to avoid scheduling your ceremony at the same time as a major event. We've had weddings delayed because the groom and all his groomsmen were glued to the Auburn-Alabama football game.

A Sunday afternoon in the fall can be a beautiful time to get married, but if half your guests are checking their fantasy football scores the entire time, that can be a downer. Plus, they are more likely rushing to be on time for the ceremony.

Even if you follow all the advice we just gave, you still cannot control other people's actions. If you know that your guests are going to be late no matter what, you may need to advance the timing on the invitations.

If you are timing your ceremony around sunset, you need to be punctual. Remember, the sunset waits for no one! A sunset ceremony is far more picturesque than getting married in the dark.

Transitioning to the reception

OK, so you got everyone to the ceremony on time, you said your vows, everyone cheered -- now how do you get dozens of people from the beach to your reception site?

The ceremony typically lasts 20 to 30 minutes. Your close family and friends will likely stick around for a few minutes to take pictures, but the rest of the group is (usually) ready to boogie.

If the folks sticking around for pictures are tough to corral, we have some crowd management techniques that we use.

Blessing Stone Ceremony

Upon request, we will have everyone walk down to the water's edge and pass out the blessing stones. This is an opportunity to make a wish and prayer for the new couple as they throw their stone into the Gulf. It makes for a great picture, it gets everyone down to the water quickly, and acts as a great way to have everyone involved in one aspect of the celebration. This is known as the Blessing Stone ceremony and takes place at the conclusion of the wedding ceremony +5 minutes down by the shoreline.

Work Backwards

Depending on the travel distance to the reception location, you will want to factor in 15-30 minutes of loading/unloading and parking. Again, these transitions will require a buffer and traffic factor. Assume people will dilly-dally, assume you will hit traffic, assume parking will be tough, someone needs to use the restroom, etc. Hopefully none of those things happen, but you don't want to have a reservation for 40 people at a restaurant and everybody is an hour late.

Often couples opt for a cocktail hour at the very beginning of the reception to incentivize guests to be punctual and is the perfect way to allow for a 'soft transition' to the reception itself!

CHAPTER 10

Food for Thought

Now we are getting to the fun part!

Once you have chosen a date and location, it's time to figure out your reception spot.

Remember -- we recommend booking the ceremony site and reception venue at the same time. You don't want to lock in your beach location without researching nearby reception locales.

Most couples discover that there are plenty of beaches that are the perfect spot for a ceremony. The thing they end up being more persnickety about is where they hold the reception.

So, what are your options?

There are three major categories when it comes to selecting a reception area, and it mostly depends on the size of your party: Restaurants (usually 2 to 35 people), reception halls (35 to 100) and hotels or resorts (100+).

The couples that we work with often fall into the restaurant or reception hall categories.

But first, a word about resorts...

If you have 120 or more guests, we will steer you toward a resort who will facilitate your entire ceremony and reception. Resorts and hotels that host weddings are geared towards larger events, and if you have the budget, they will make it happen.

Want to ride down the aisle on a baby elephant? If you got the cash, saddle up.

But here is where we will offer one word of caution: Holding your wedding at a hotel or resort and expecting to find any deals is like looking for the cheap beer vendor at the Super Bowl.

They just aren't there.

Don't get me wrong, you can have a beautiful wedding at a hotel or resort, but these are best suited for couples with a 'loose' budget.

The hotel and resort prices help keep us in business. We have worked with couples who, when they realized their special day at a resort was going to set them back more than $30,000 (not including travel costs, dress, honeymoon, etc.), ditched the resort and hired us.

But -- if you are set on having more than 100 guests, a resort may be your best option. They are geared to have all guests attended to at all times...you just have to pay for it.

Restaurants

If your beach wedding has 35 or fewer guests (35 is not a hard-and-fast cutoff, more of a general rule) then a restaurant is your best option for the reception.

A few things you may have noticed about restaurants: They have tables and chairs. They are fairly decorated. They have food preparation facilities (also known as a kitchen) on site. They have wait staff, bars and some even have live music.

Why is this important? Because all of those are things that you would otherwise need to bring when you rent out a reception hall or convert some other space into your reception area, they are already provided.

You can create your own reception site, but it's good to consider just how much heavy lifting it is going to take plus those additional rental costs. Sometimes, you are starting from scratch...

Restaurants are the ideal spot for smaller receptions as they are already in the food services business. Depending on the size of your group and location, some have private dining rooms where you can have a family-style meal served, toast the bride and the groom, and then leave without having to worry about the clean-up.

However, if you have (roughly) 40 or more guests, your group is too large for most restaurants, and it actually begins to become more expensive than it would be to reserve a banquet hall or convert another space into a reception area. Plus, you have the added benefit of a private space.

Reception Venue or Converting a space

If you have between 40 and 100 guests, you will want to rent out a facility to use as your reception area.

This is the ideal option for couples that need to stick to their budget, but also want the bigger wedding and privacy of their 'own' reception hall. With this number of guests, you begin to see cost savings the more people you have.

When converting a space into a reception area, keep in mind that you are typically renting an empty room that you will need to turn into your reception hall. That means bringing in chairs, tables, linens, lighting, decor, flowers, and a sound system. You will need to hire a caterer and set up a bar. You may need to rent a 'bathroom trailer.' In short, it can be a lot of work and quite costly, not to mention making all these arrangements from out of town.

This is not the case with Affordable Banquet, our very own reception hall on St Pete Beach, complete with Chiavari chairs, tables, linens, lighting, and a sound system. There is even a closet full of coastal decor, signs, candles, etc. that couples can use for the day to make the reception venue their own. This facility is ready to go, just add food and a DJ! However, this is the exception...most venues are a blank canvas or offer decor provided by the managing company for a price. If you end up bringing some of your own decor/goods for a one-time use, please feel free to leave on-site and another future couple will gladly appreciate the wedding gesture!

Don't discount VA halls, city and municipally owned spaces and pavilions. These too, with a little bit of creative flair, can provide the perfect venue or space for the reception at a fraction of the cost of a full-on reception hall.

Creating your own reception space is one part of the wedding that many couples love. It gives them a chance to put their unique stamp on the event, with decor, music and toasts that match their personalities. You'll have more privacy than you would at a restaurant, and you won't be sharing your space with strangers who popped in to grab a burger and find themselves in the midst of a wedding party.

If renting a reception venue is the route that makes the most sense for you, we've got the connections and we can steer you toward some of the best venues on the Gulf Coast.

One last note, most halls/venues rent by the day, hourly, or time block (For example 6 or 8 hours). So be prepared and factor in setup time/tear down following the event. If you only have 6 hours total, this leaves 1-2 hours for setup and 1 hour for take down (and only 3-4 hours for the entire ceremony and reception). Full-day rental is the ultimate option if available.

And remember -- on the day of, take a deep breath, sit back, and enjoy all the time, preparation, and planning that went into your special day. Expect to encounter some hiccups, but these should not prevent you from having the most magical day.

That doesn't mean a catastrophe is imminent, but florists get lost, PA systems can have static, weather is too hot or too cold, an electrical outlet isn't in the right location, or that slide show of the bride and groom didn't save properly on your laptop.

Whatever it is, there are going to be some hiccups throughout the day that you should be prepared for mentally. When converting a space into your reception area, there are even more variables in the day's equation, so be ready to roll with the unexpected.

Catering and Food Options

About half of the couples that we do weddings for here at Gulf Beach Weddings® had their reception at a restaurant. As we've said, that is the optimal choice if you have 35 or fewer guests.

But what if you are going to have a larger ceremony? The couples that go this route will need to hire a caterer for their event. We have connections with the best caterers up and down Florida's Gulf Coast, and we can help you put together a reception that leaves your guests stuffed and happy.

A few things to keep in mind:

Folks who haven't been to a wedding in a while might have a skewed impression of what the typical reception meal looks like. Movies and television often show plated dinners, where guests are served "the chicken" or "the fish" as part of a meal with several courses.

The truth is, no one does plated meals anymore, and that is a good thing.

Rather than a dry chicken breast that has been sitting on a plate for 30 minutes before it is placed in front of you, most caterers set up buffet stations with food that is marinating in a sauce and gets tastier with time.

Plus, a formal meal served by waiters doesn't really fit with our laid-back beach vibe. You want your guests up and mingling, piling their plate high with the delicious options you've picked out.

As you work with your caterer on creating the perfect menu, you may think you already know exactly what you want to serve your guests. Maybe your mouth still waters when you think back to the mashed potato bar at a friend's wedding, or the fondue station at your aunt's wedding when you were seven that seemed like something out of "Charlie and the Chocolate Factory."

Here is our advice: Listen to the Caterer

Most of them have a handful of dishes that they have mastered. They know exactly how to scale the recipe based on the number of guests, how to ensure it comes out at the right temperature and consistency.

Most of all, they have received enormous amounts of feedback on what large crowds like. They know what's popular, and what dishes they end up throwing away because no one will touch it. It is a constant feedback loop, and you would be wise to listen if they try to steer you away from a certain dish.

As a rule, don't ask for something that is not on the menu. If you ask them to try something new for your big day, you may not like the results.

Also, remember that everything is prepared off site, so opt for a menu that travels well.

Pulled pork, stuffed mushrooms, lobster mac and cheese, brisket with mashed potatoes, chicken cordon bleu, Mediterranean pasta's or anything 'stuffed' - are popular dishes that taste *better* after sitting in a warming container during the drive from the caterer's kitchen to the reception site. Fried foods and premade sandwiches get soggy during transport, and dishes with a lot of components like eggs benedict rarely survive the drive.

—

Catering prices can begin as low as $18-20 per person. But if you want filet, lobster, sea bass or tuna, expect to pay more.

In recent years, we have received more and more questions about food trucks. Well, let's talk about it.

A word about food trucks:

Food trucks have exploded in popularity over the past decade. They are the charming spawn of the Great Recession, when out-of-work chefs took to the streets to sell gourmet bar-be-cue, sushi, and tacos.

And while we have nothing against a good taco served out of an old school bus after a night out with friends, we do not recommend a food truck for your reception.

Wedding receptions are what caterers do. They know how to serve large crowds and how to put together a menu to please an array of palates. Their entire business model is based on feeding many hungry people at once.

Food trucks have a totally different mode of operating. Most food trucks are not set up to serve 50 people that show up at once. Your guests may end up spending half the entire reception waiting in line for food. They also are likely to have a limited menu.

The explosion in popularity of food trucks has also led to a decline in quality. Cities like Austin, Texas and Portland, Oregon -- both foodie heavens -- are where food trucks got their reputation as Michelin 5-Star restaurants on wheels. But just because food is being served out of a van doesn't mean it is good or fresh. We've seen food truck receptions where the guests waited an hour in line for a sub-par meal that cost more than what a caterer would have charged. If you do plan to go this route, make sure they have a local business license and are registered with the Department of Professional Regulation (for Florida) having the applicable Catering License.

Bottom line: If someone is good at serving large crowds at once (which is what you will most likely want for your reception), they are not doing it out of a truck.

Let them eat cake!

It's going to be one of the sweetest days of your life, so bring on dessert!

More and more couples are being creative with dessert - options like cupcakes, doughnuts, and ice cream. Instead of a traditional wedding cake, they'll have a dessert or 'candy' station. This fits with the non-traditional nature of a beach wedding.

But -- many couples still want the traditional wedding cake, so here are a few pointers for you:

❖ Bakers typically have one or two flavors that they can do perfectly, and you are paying for their secret sauce. For example, one local caterer specializes in a marble cheesecake, and they are known throughout the area for this delicacy. In other words, you don't want your wedding day to be an experiment.

❖ A word of warning -- wedding cakes can be expensive because you are not just paying for a cake. You are paying for the skill and artistry that goes into creating something both tasty and beautiful. There will probably be some customization. You need someone who knows how to transport large baked goods. You need it to be safely made. And you want it to be delicious.

❖ Cakes are priced on a per-slice basis. If your caterer serves the cake (even if you buy the cake from a separate baker), you will get charged a cake-cutting fee. This is standard throughout the industry.

❖ If you are on a tight budget, the beloved Florida based grocery chain Publix is your solution. Publix-baked cakes are delicious, and we've never seen anyone unhappy with a piece of Publix cake in hand. More and more, their selections rival serious bakers.

❖ If you end up bringing your own cake, make sure it stays refrigerated in the hours leading up to being served. Remember, it is Florida, and you don't want the icing to liquefy when you cut into the cake because it's been baking under the Florida sun for the last few hours. The best location to ensure the cake is safe is the restaurant or reception venue, these locations typically have very large refrigerators and are used to this request.

To smear, or not to smear?

Should we smear cake in each other's face?

Witnessing thousands of cake-cutting ceremonies, there is no one-size-fits-all answer to this. For some couples, it is a silly and lighthearted moment.

Generally, these couples don't go overboard, and they don't seem hell-bent on smearing icing all over their new spouse's face.

But, trust me, we've seen it go sideways.

Brides in tears, cakes ruined, and a couple's first fight coming mere hours after the ceremony. It's fun in the beginning...but turns messy quickly!

Keep in mind that – most likely – the bride has spent hours preparing her waterproof makeup. You two just proclaimed your lifelong commitment to one another in a sacred ceremony. Is it really the best time to start a food fight?

As a happily married man who did not slam my wife's face into our wedding cake, I might say no. As a spectator, I might say yes.

If you do decide to go the food fight route, make sure you keep it civil.

CHAPTER 11

Sunny Days are Here Again

Being a meteorologist on the Gulf Coast of Florida has got to be an easy gig. From Destin to Tampa, Florida's West Coast has some of the most predictable seasons in the country.

Is it July? It's going to be hot, and the chances are high there will be a brief but intense thunderstorm in the late afternoon. Is it November? Expect temperatures to be in the 70's, and you can leave your umbrella at home.

Outside of hurricane season (we'll get to that shortly), weather forecasting on the Gulf Coast is as easy as looking at the calendar.

That's good news for you as you plan your beach wedding because you can predict with reasonable accuracy what the temperature will be, how likely it is to rain and what time the sun will set.

But what happens if it rains?

The Tampa Bay region has two basic seasons: A hot and rainy season from June through September and a mild and dry season from October through May. The rainy season is most intense in the summer months, with two thirds of the annual rainfall occurring in July, August, and September. This herein also lies a secret...the fall has less precipitation than the spring, even though spring is considered 'Wedding Season.'

The afternoon showers during the rainy season are as intense as they are brief. Unlike northern cities where you may have a gray and gloomy day leading up to a rainstorm, the Tampa Bay region is known for hot and sunny summer days punctuated by a brief and dramatic rainstorm known as a "rain band."

Typically, during a rain band, the sky opens and there will be a 5 to 10 minute-long vigorous downpour. Then, the sun comes out.

Because rain is so predictable in the summer months, our wedding pros are experts at navigating your special day through an afternoon thunderstorm.

So, what should you expect if clouds start gathering just before your ceremony? First, don't freak out.

1 - Equipment

All the equipment that we provide is waterproof and designed for the hot sun, water, salt air, and direct sunlight day in, day out. That means the chairs, the sound system, the arch – all of it can withstand the daily deluge. Our staff will have plenty of towels on hand to dry everything off and an umbrella for the bride.

2 – Weather Forecasts

We will usually have a pretty good sense if rain is coming, so our wedding pros may tell you to pump the brakes on putting out the non-rain-proof accoutrements (programs, fans, flowers, etc) if it looks like a shower is imminent. We use a host of resources: current & forecasted radar, aviation forecasts, hourly forecasts, recent weather and draw on a 'gut' weather option combining all of the above.

3 – Backup Locations

We know all the best spots to ride out the storm.

Many of the beaches where we perform ceremonies have pavilions where you and your guests can gather if the skies open up. Or we can adjust the time slightly and try to thread the needle according to the hourly forecasts.

There are two unexpected benefits to an intense downpour right before your ceremony: First, it clears out all the sunbathers, so you are more likely to have the beach to yourself. Secondly, the moisture in the air at sunset is a photographer's dream. The most dramatic wedding photographs almost always come right after a storm. Pinks, blues, orange, red and green commonly fill the sky and sunbeams pierce the clouds for a truly remarkable backdrop (perhaps even a rainbow).

What about weather outside of the typical daily downpour?

We monitor the weather obsessively, and if it looks like inclement weather is going to interrupt your big day we can adjust. We don't make any decisions longer than 24 hours in advance as weather patterns can shift and forecasts are often unreliable outside of this time frame. Changing the time, day or location of your ceremony is not something you want to do unless absolutely necessary and must be done with ample time for the vendors, setup crew, and coordinators to adjust.

If it looks like bad weather is inevitable for the day of your ceremony, we can help you move the wedding up a day in advance or to the following day. There are no guarantees that we can do this because you are likely working with multiple vendors, but we do everything we can in this regard.

This is one of the primary benefits to having a mid-week ceremony, as there's more flexibility for everyone involved.

The beauty of a Gulf beach wedding is that your guests are in town for a couple days surrounding the ceremony. They don't have all the obligations of being at home, so shifting the wedding by one day or one hour doesn't throw everyone's schedule into disarray.

What about the worst-case scenario?

If the weather is bad for the entire day and we can't reschedule, we can still facilitate an outdoor ceremony under a nearby pavilion. This truly is a worst-case scenario but does happen 4 to 5 times per year. There's just no way to know 3, 6, 12 months out in advance which days God has chosen to add more 'good luck' to the couple's special day!

Insurance options – cost and what does it cover?

We strongly encourage couples to have a true back-up option and further purchase 'Event Insurance' for your wedding. Over the years, the coverage has been more and more defined specific to a 'Wedding Event' and covering a host of items: deposits to vendors, out of pocket expenses, stolen/lost jewelry and venue cancellation. Policy premiums are largely determined by the following: length of the event, number of guests, coverage amount, property and/or liquor liability, cancellation/postponement, and deposit amounts. Pricing typically starts in the mid $100's and goes up from there. Be sure to read the fine print as these policies are designed for catastrophic loss, not an inconvenience. Travelers®, Wedsure®, and WedSafe® are a great place to start!

CHAPTER 12

Congratulations! This is just the beginning...

All the advice that is packed in this book comes from experience.

I'm always hesitant to say, "We've seen it all" because I don't want to invite fate to throw me a curveball at the next ceremony. But we have seen plenty in the thousands of beach weddings we have performed since 2011.

This performance and experience have trained us to be ready for anything, and we have become pros at anticipating problems and making them go away.

We know how to sweet talk the drunk into moving his stuff down the beach, so he is not in your guests' line of sight. We know how to mobilize your group when they are dilly dallying, and it is time to get pictures as the sun sets. We know the people to take care of because they play a key role in some aspect of your day - - the front desk clerks at your hotel, the servers at your reception hall and the bus driver transporting your guests.

99% of our ceremonies go off without a hitch, let alone something that would be worthy of making it into this book. But every wedding will have some unexpected twist that you can't perfectly anticipate.

If you have made it this far, you are probably thinking one of two things:

Either "Wow this guy knows everything about beach weddings, I'm going to take his advice."

Or "Wow, throwing a beach wedding sounds harder than I thought. I am going to hire Gulf Beach Weddings®."

We are happy with either outcome.

The knowledge we have accumulated in over ten years of executing beach weddings needs to be used -- there is no point in knowing that the ringbearer should carry a decoy ring to prevent the heartache of losing the real one in the sand and not sharing that valuable lesson with couples in the planning process.

If you learned from our experience and this book helps you navigate the process of saying "I do" on the beach, we would love to hear from you.

We want to know what was most helpful, and what you wish you had known ahead of time.

And if, as you have read this, you've decided you want to trust the experts with your big day, give us a call. We aren't bragging when we say there is literally no one else in the world with as much experience with beach weddings as our team.

This book is designed to be a crash course in the basics, but there is no replacement for the decades of combined experience that our experts bring. If you want to tap into our expertise to ensure that your wedding day is perfect, let's talk. Feel free to call (727) 475-2272, (850) 898-0600 or email our offices at info@gulfbeachweddings.com.

Most importantly, marriage is not to be taken lightly – there are items apart of the ceremony that can have a certain 'cynicism' in this regard. However, we highly recommend pre-marital counseling, recurrent marriage retreats, celebrating the ups and downs as you are in a forever partnership with a life mate. One particularly valuable experience is the WinShape Foundation®, Retreat at Mount Barry. This is the ideal location to focus on your marriage and each other for a weekend – nestled in the beauty of Rome, GA. I can speak from prior experience, this is another 'must do' as you navigate married life.

Once again, Congratulations on your upcoming dream beach wedding and thank you for reading to the end. We will see you out on the beach!

APPENDIX & HYPERLINKS

Below are helpful links and resources to assist in planning the perfect Gulf Beach Wedding!

Gulf Beach Weddings® - Homepage:
https://gulfbeachweddings.com/

Download a Digital Copy:
https://gulfbeachweddings.com/guide

Interactive Beach WeddingStudio®:
https://gulfbeachweddings.com/product/beach-wedding-builder/

Perfect Beach Questionnaire:
https://gulfbeachweddings.com/beach-ratings-form/

About Us:
https://gulfbeachweddings.com/about-us/

Reviews & Testimonials:
https://gulfbeachweddings.com/reviews/

FAQ & Common Questions:
https://gulfbeachweddings.com/faq-common-questions/

Ceremony Timeline:
https://gulfbeachweddings.com/ceremony-timeline/

Free Wedding Website:
https://gulfbeachweddings.com/custom-wedding-website/

Wedding Ceremony & Vow – Templates:
https://gulfbeachweddings.com/wedding-ceremony-and-vows/

Blog, Articles, & Posts:
https://gulfbeachweddings.com/blog/

Hotel & Lodging:
https://gulfbeachweddings.com/booking/

Tampa Beach Ratings:
https://gulfbeachweddings.com/beach-ratings-2/

Destin Beach Ratings:
https://gulfbeachweddings.com/emerald-coast-beach-ratings/

Copyright Free Music & Video:
https://www.pond5.com/

WinShape Foundation®, Retreat at Mount Berry:
https://welcome.winshape.org/

Chair Sash Palette:
https://gulfbeachweddings.com/wp-content/uploads/2020/01/GBW_Chair-Sash-Colors.pdf

Arch Fabric Palette:
https://gulfbeachweddings.com/wp-content/uploads/2020/01/GBW_Arch-Sash-Colors.pdf

Unity Sand Palette:
https://gulfbeachweddings.com/wp-content/uploads/2020/06/Unity-Sand-Palette-2020-GBW-.pdf

US Service Animals® - Online Service Animal Registration: https://usserviceanimals.org

Sample Program:
https://gulfbeachweddings.com/sample-program/

Affordable Banquet:
https://gulfbeachweddings.com/affordable-banquet/

Made in the USA
Columbia, SC
29 September 2024

43298113R00065